Omnibus Press
London/New York/Sydney/Tokyo/Cologne

LESTER BANGS

Published by Omnibus Press
London/New York/Sydney/
Tokyo/Cologne

*Produced by
Delilah Communications Ltd.
New York*

To Napoleon XIV
for Side B

Omnibus Press

Distributed by Book Sales Limited, London and Sydney.
ISBN 0 86001 711 7 UK Order No. OP 40690

Designed by George Delmerico

Printed in England by Panda Press Ltd., Haverhill, Suffolk.

2 3 4 5 6 7 8 9 10

First of all, thanks to Stephanie Bennett (tough cop), Jeannie Sakol (con cop), Karen Moline (the most indefatigable and possibly most physically beautiful woman in New York City, and my pal), Madeleine Morel, Kathy Braker, George Delmerico, and anybody else with anything to do with Delilah Communications, Ltd., without whom none of this would have happened; and especially to Jeannie and Karen, my immediate editors, for their patience, their tolerance of my excesses and their general rock 'n' roll sensibilities rare among literary people anywhere. To my agent, Keith Korman, for keeping a sharp eye peeled re my interests at all times, and being a great Jim Morrison fan; to Fran Pelzman, for introducing me to Karen in the first place and other things; to Diana Clapton, for moral and chemical support; to Kathy Miller, Chris Moss and the couple dozen Catholic High School Girls in Trouble, and especially to Vera for proper radical perspectives and the Musicale; to Billy Altman and John Morthland, for general wisecracks and good advice; and to Debra Rae Cohen for crib notes beyond the call of duty and being so supportive when you didn't even know you were.

L.B., Feb. 16, 1980

Poor Dagwood, Dead and Gone

A BRIEF CHRONOLOGUE

Left Me Here To Sing His Song

JANUARY 1977: I had just reviewed a group off New York City's CBGB-nascent punk rock circuit called Blondie for the *Village Voice*. All my friends had said they were a waste, but I found their first album a charming, even inspiring piece of American rock 'n' roll from traditions as diverse as early Sixties girl groups, Question Mark and the Mysterians, and the Velvet Underground. So, under the title "Blondie is More Fun," I gave it what probably amounted to a rave review; in those days, when seemingly everybody else around except the Ramones and Dictators were taking themselves *so* seriously, Blondie were refreshing. One day the phone rang; it was the band themselves, calling me up to thank me. We chatted a bit, and at one point I asked them what else besides rock they were into.

"Japanese culture," one of them said.

"You mean like Yukio Mishima?" I asked.

"No," they said, "we mean like Japanese monster movies!"

Not long after that Private Stock, their record company, sent me a big poster of Deborah Harry, their lead singer, in a see-thru blouse. I duly tacked it up on the wall, though even at the time I had to admit I didn't find it that sexy, and my girlfriend, far from taking offense at this bit of sexist exploitation, just thought she looked sad.

MARCH 1977: I got to see Blondie for the first time, opening for Iggy Pop at the Palladium in New York, one of their first gigs in a big hall. They were all kind of clumsy out there, not least the girl lead singer, miniskirt, California GTO-cruisin' sunglasses and all. But just like their record they were fun in the flesh, and in fact it was perhaps the band's very awkwardness that made them endearing. After Iggy'd chilled our hearts and blown our brains out the door with that one wild shout that ended "T.V. Eye" alone, we all came away filled with his fire but also thinking and talking about how utterly cute without the slightest hint of the cloying Blondie were. My crowd, rock critics of all shapes and sizes and eras, were unanimous in feeling really kind of filially/fraternally supportive of them. They felt like spiritual rock 'n' roll family, which for all his anomic maelstroms was something one could never quite say about Iggy, unless he was, perhaps, three generations of ghosts, howling deep into the wells and crevasses of the Seventies to see just who else might have fallen down there.

OCTOBER 1977: I was in London, staying at author/record producer/disc jockey Charlie Gillett's house, recuperating from six days on the road with the Clash. He mentioned one day that Blondie were playing somewhere in town that night, and asked me if he should check them out. I gave them a big buildup, and he came back that night almost a little miffed at me for wasting his time on something he considered so lame. A day or two later I shared his Sunday afternoon *Honky Tonk* radio show with Blondie. They were about half fried and half exhilarated: fried because of all the touring, exhilarated because their single "In the Flesh" had gone Number One in Australia. Deborah Harry, the lead singer, must in fact have had one of the most convoluted cases of jet-lag of all time, because she had just finished flying from New York City to Australia with their manager Peter Leeds to give interviews and promote their records, and then direct from Australia to London to join the rest of them for more European touring. Interestingly enough, she seemed less wearied by all this frenetic career-goosing than the guys in the group. The first thing she did was make Charlie put on a record of Australian pigmy music recorded under the mud of the deepest Outback, "Because I wanta start helpin' pay back some of our fans in Australia for makin' us big stars there first, so here's some of *their* music."

I was experiencing a little difficulty in bearing up under assault by that many pigmies at once myself, and I'm a connoisseur of obnoxious music. I looked over at Charlie to see how he thought this matched up to the Drifters; he looked like he'd just swallowed a toad after losing about three pints of blood. Then I glanced at the turntable: the cut looked like it was about 15 minutes long. Debbie seemed to be in heaven; maybe, as many said of the MC5's *Kick Out the Jams*, you just hadda be there. The rest of the band was just sort of wandering around the studio distractedly in their black leather jackets; they all looked like they wished they were at the Gem Spa on St. Mark's Place instead.

About six minutes into the bush, Charlie finally had to take the little chooglers off before the skin started to peel spontaneously from his body.

"Well, that's enough of that," he said, and the rest of the show was divided among the Blondies, who played all their favorite current New Wave singles (Penetration, Richard Hell, Ramones, etc.) and, at the very end, me (Eno, Ray Charles, Richard Hell, Robert Quine hype). Charlie also did a brief interview with

Debbie, who tensed up visibly the instant the show changed to that from a sort of record party, and he certainly didn't win any points with her by mentioning the Wind in the Willows, a hippie-folkie group she was in in 1968, thus inferring her age which is something she's been uptight about ever since I've known her, though he was too much of a gentleman to press her on it.

On another topic she was not so much touchy as adamant. "Is Blondie a punk band?" asked Charlie.

"Definitely not," responded Debbie, though she didn't seem offended by the suggestion. "We play *power-pop!*"

Meanwhile, whenever the records were playing, I chatted with the band. None of them seemed particularly happy to be in England/Europe for the first time—they were experiencing the usual acclimatization process American bands undergo when they storm over there for debut tours, *always* thinking they're gonna be the Beatles in reverse and getting undone a few nerves a day by the dreary weather, the steady diet of things like bangers and mash, the drafty hotel rooms, phones in them that might work and might not, etc. Once they figure out it's not Carnaby Street and *Blow-Up* but a basically worthless country where it's advisable to stay drunk like most of the natives, they generally do all right. Apparently not quite broken in yet, Chris Stein, Debbie's boyfriend and co-leader of the band with her, told me: "All their groups but the Sex Pistols, the Clash and maybe a couple others stink. The longer we're over here the more nationalistic we get."

Though I had been diverted by matters Clash, I was a little surprised to hear him voice these sentiments, inasmuch as I'd gathered that England, both press and audiences, had responded fairly favorably to the group. I was just beginning to learn that the English and American (then almost entirely concentrated in New York at the eternal sleaze-haven Max's Kansas City, and a former folk club and wino hangout down Bleecker and Bowery called CBGB's) punk contingents were hardly destined to be a united front: all the Limeys thought the CBGB's bands were a lot of spoiled suburban-affluent dilettante junkies, and all the Americans thought the London safety-pin and bondage-trousers brigade were a self-righteously "political," speed-nattering mob of pogoing poseurs who were all too short, no doubt owing to their hideous culinary practices. I loved it all myself, but running into Blondie reminded me how badly I wanted to be back home myself, the sweet chitterings of the jackhammers wafting up from Sixth Avenue, sounding not unlike and possibly better than whichever new band might happen to be playing that night at CBGB's, where for once in my life I'd found a "scene" I actually felt comfortable in: a dogpound with an open-door policy to brain-damage, literal physical deformity, black leather jackets lending many a wimpy li'l thing the proper menacing carapace, and teenage heffalumps for whom beer was the Grail.

FEBRUARY 1978: I got Blondie's second album, *Plastic Letters*, in the mail, and was surprised to find that I didn't care for it much. But even more disconcerting was the press kit that came with it, in which a group that I'd considered the current quintessence of fun came off surprisingly solemn, sullen even, not a smiling face in the bunch. I began to wonder what was going through their heads.

DESTINY IN THEIR SHADES: THE RAMONES, CLEM, DEBBIE, CHRIS,

FEBRUARY 1979: I was in a rock 'n' roll band myself, and my lead guitarist and I were driving to a rehearsal when suddenly we heard this blast of hard-sell hysteria coming over the radio: a commercial for *Parallel Lines*, the new album by—*"BLONDIE!!!"* We snickered. These were the same people we had hung out with around the bar all summer '77. We were jealous.

RAMONES AIDE-DE-CAMP ARTURO VEGA AND GARY AT MOTHER'S ON 23RD ST., 1975.

SPRING 1979: "Heart of Glass" was the Number One record in the country, and a guitarist friend had called up and wondered with me whether this might mean that more extreme New Wave bands like Richard Hell and the Voidoids might have a chance in the marketplace after all. Meanwhile, a local FM station was using the song in its own TV ad. One Friday night after a rehearsal my band all hunkered down to get high and watch *The Midnight Special*. It turned out to be an all-disco show, hosted by none other than … *"BLONDIE!!!"* They did "Heart of Glass" while discoids hustled by with mock-S&M moves. Debbie's stage moves didn't seem to have changed much in the two years since the Palladium gig with Iggy. "She's the Barbie Benton of punk," I cracked as she waved a veil in front of her face. Everybody laughed. We were still jealous.

SUMMER 1979: "Heart of Glass" had come and gone, though *Parallel Lines* was still on the charts, where it remained well into 1980. I was no longer jealous, my band having broken up, but I was surprised to see Chris Stein on a panel with Brian Eno and several other representatives of contemporary music's outer fringes at a weeklong New Music, New York Festival at Manhattan's Kitchen Center for Music, Video and Dance. We shared a cab uptown afterwards, and, in the middle of some bitter comments from Chris about a recent profile of the band in *Rolling Stone* which I hadn't read, I said not with malice but slight perplexity: "I never thought of Blondie as members of the avant-garde."

"Oh, yes, we are," Chris hastily assured me. Eno nodded his assent. The best I could have come up with at that point would have been something along the lines of "Gee …"

OCTOBER 1979: Deborah Harry on the cover of *US* magazine. *Eat to the Beat* came in the mail for review. The cover showed six faces as solemn as the ones in the press kit for *Plastic Letters*. While I liked some of the cuts a lot, others didn't so much turn me off as escape me entirely. I still couldn't see that I was listening to anything more than a decent pop band, whatever any Brian Eno thought, though many of the lyrics and little twists in the arrangements of some songs, particularly on the second side, did suggest that at least they were avant-garde enough to be obscure. On the final cut Debbie spat over and over again: "I'm not living in the real world." Was something seriously wrong with these people or was it that I just didn't understand them?

FEBRUARY 1980: Just how popular is Blondie? They're featured on the cover of *Cash Box*, which reports that *Parallel Lines*, selling 7 million copies worldwide and gone Platinum here, is still on the album chart after 72 weeks, and that *Eat to the Beat* made it to #14, and that "Dreaming," the first single from it, hit Top Twenty at least. Can cheesecake keep you on the charts for 72 weeks? Somehow I doubt it.

Growing Up Streaked

Deborah Harry was born in Miami, Florida to an unlisted mother. When she was three months old she was adopted by Richard and Catherine Harry, and she grew up in Hawthorne, New Jersey. Her parents now run a gift shop in Cooperstown, N.Y. Debbie has remained very family oriented: her mother told *Rolling Stone* that the only time Debbie missed Christmas at home was when she was on tour in Australia, and laughingly, that "She's the one that got homesick at camp."

According to Debbie, the first songs she remembers from childhood are "The Lollipop Tree" ("I think Burl Ives sang it.") and "Froggie Went A-Courtin'."

She made her singing debut in a sixth-grade play, twirled baton, joined the fencing club, student council, yearbook staff, and variety show in high school, and graduated from Hawthorne High in 1963, career ambition "Undecided."

She looked well-scrubbed in her yearbook, but clearly other things were brewing. "I was sort of weird," she told one interviewer of her high school days. "I had my hair bleached white all over with a vegetable coloring and I used to wear black every day. I was an art student."

She was even more solemn in her description of teen rebellion: "I was destined to be an artist even then. I practiced putting on makeup a lot. I used to study it carefully and *practice* everything.... I made a lot of mistakes; sometimes I'd walk out of the house looking like a ghoul and not really know it. One time in eighth grade my mother wasn't home; so I went upstairs and started fooling around. When I went back to school after lunch, no one would talk to me. Everybody went to one side of the lounge, and I was all by myself, practically in tears, with beauty marks all over my face...."

"I must have had ten or twelve different colors of hair. I started with streaks, and then it gradually turned orange. Later it was turning up platinum."

Her parents tried sending her to a finishing school for future corporation wives, but it was, after all, the mid-Sixties, and New Jersey is, after all, right next to New York, which has meant "the Village" for generations of young people who pop out of high school practically spuming Artistic Destiny.

Debbie arrived in the first flush of Hippie, and soon found herself in the Wind in the Willows, a sort of woodsy Tolkienish band who even put out one album on Capitol back in 1968. Produced by Artie Kornfeld, who went on to more glorious and profitable ventures (like Woodstock), it flopped and the group broke up. The cover's still worth a gander just to note the woman who would one day be referred to as the "punk Garbo" down there among all those beards and caftans, a timid little thing with mousy brown hair.

Not Quite "Barefoot in the Park": Max's, Dope, Stillettoes & Strange Boys in Blue Eyeshadow

When the group broke up, Debbie almost went down in the maelstrom that was the urban end of the hippie dream. Just about everybody else in the East Village (and, it sometimes seemed, in the New York rock scene during the Sixties) was into drugs.

For a while Debbie worked at the Playboy Club as a Bunny, and her memories of the experience vary:

New York Rocker, 1976: It's pretty disgusting work.

Three years later in 1979 *Playboy*: It's a great job for a girl who wants to make a lot of money and doesn't know what else to do.

Oh well.

Around the same time she got a job at Max's Kansas City, waiting tables for superstars from the worlds of rock and Warhol. Again, her recollections vary:

Penthouse, ca. '79: It was fun being so naive and young ... to just stand around and look at Andy Warhol, Viva, Ultra Violet, Jane Fonda, James Coburn, Roger Vadim, the Jefferson Airplane, Janis Joplin, Jimi Hendrix, you name it. I'd be there every night and watch Alice Cooper go up and down. When I finished work, I'd go upstairs and dance my ass off, What a great time I had! What an education I got!

New York Rocker ca. '76: I used to cry a lot then generally. They were very frustrating people to wait on.

"Everybody was on drugs then," Ritty Dodge, who worked with Debbie at Max's, told *Penthouse*. "But nobody talked about it ... Debbie looked then, I thought, like a nice Polish girl—very corn-fed, with long, dirty-blonde hair. Everyone I knew loved her ... but she was *never* one of the ones who passed out in the bathroom.... she had to have been a little naive, I think, a little out of her depth."

About this time in 1972, the New York Dolls unleashed something on New York not unlike what happened later with the Ramones, Patti Smith and Television at CBGB. Marty Thau, who managed the Dolls and later Suicide, and has remained friends with Debbie and the other people in Blondie to this day, describes meeting her: "When I first saw her I was amazed at how beautiful she was. But she was very quiet, and later on I learned from her that that was during the period of time when she was very frightened and kinda paranoid about a lot of things. Like she phrased it, at one point she was just there but she couldn't speak to anybody, she was too fragile.

"Later word got back to me that she was a singer in the Stillettoes, and they were very good. I never saw them perform, but I did get a lot of feedback from people who said, 'Hey, Debbie has this group and can sing and she's really beautiful. This group should really be caught to see if there was something that could be done with them.' But I was involved full time with the Dolls."

WITH LANCE LOUD AND ROOMMATE AT MAX'S.

Later Debbie would describe her initial hookup with the Stillettoes: "I worked as a beautician for a while. I heard that Elda (Gentile) Stilletto and Holly Woodlawn and Diane had a girl trio called Pure Garbage. I became obsessed with this. I saw Elda one night at Max's and I said, 'Oh, I heard you have a trio. I'd love to come down and hear it.' And she said, 'Well, it broke up.' And I said, 'Well, if you ever want another singer, call me.' And that's how I got back into doing it.

"Elda, me and Rosie Ross were the original Stillettoes. Tony Ingrassia was our director. He worked on the songs with us, projecting a mood through a song, stage tricks to give us a cohesive look. He and Elda used to fight about the image. She wanted *True Confessions* trash, tacky."

Well, why not? This was the time and place where camp and rock meshed most comfortably, most of the New York groups being more than a little influenced by things like Theatre of the Ridiculous, a camp company still around today who put on plays like Jackie Curtis' *Vain Victory* (in which Debbie had a role: Juicy Lucy, a "chorus girl"), and which has since petered down influence-wise to safer, more adulter-

Overleaf:
THE STILLETTOES'
FINAL DAYS: CHRIS,
DEBBIE, ELDA STILLETTO,
ROSIE ROSS AND FRED
SMITH GIVE GLAM SCAM
ONE MORE SCHMEAR
ON BILL W. DOLLS,
CLUB 82, 1974.

Above: **IN JACKIE CURTIS' "VAIN VICTORY": DOUBLE PANCAKE, HOLD THE COLDCREAM.**

ated mass-cult trash like *The Rocky Horror Show*. Elda has recalled that the early Stillettoes' best song was something called "Dracula, What Did You Do to My Mother," and that they wore "green crosses and skull eyeglasses that we bought on 42nd Street."

They played a little dump called the Boburn Tavern on 28th St., as well as Club 82, famed for its dieseldyke bartenders and as the place where the Dolls performed one night in (not very high, and under duress from lead singer David Johansen) drag. According to Elda, they were starting to get a following, and before the band broke up even David and Angie Bowie Themselves came down one night to check out the haps. In 1979, Elda was something less than sanguine in her memories of Debbie: "She used to make me swear to God that I'd never tell anybody she sang with that other band, Wind in the Willows. I didn't know about it till months after we started working together. It was a very hard-rock thing that was going on then, and anything that seemed to be going against it—I think she was afraid people might be turned off. She wrote pretty lyrics, like 'In the Flesh,' that she had no faith in. She was so unconfident; we'd go, 'Come on, this is beautiful,' but she wouldn't admit it. I'm very hard-edged, but she has a softness, a bubbliness, that she just pushed down."

Elda was also not too happy about the fact that, as the sisters Tish and Snooky Bellomo (who were soon to work with Debbie themselves) describe it: "Elda let Debbie in the band, and then after a while Debbie left and took the band with her, leaving Elda out in the cold when it was her band to begin with."

Jimmy Wyndbrandt of the Miamis, who was also on the scene at the time, marks it down to "pretty much irreconcilable differences between Debbie and Elda. They were getting kinda successful even though they hadn't played very much—a three-girl thing hadn't happened in a long time. They broke up I believe because of rivalries; everybody had different ideas of where it was going. Chris and Debbie were already thinking about what they wanted to do musically, and Elda's very into theatrics."

If nothing else, then, Debbie did get two things from the Stillettoes: a band and Chris, who had been brought down to see them one night by his roommate Eric Emerson, who was seeing Elda at the time.

16

egend will have it, as legend so often does, that Deb and Chris' eyes met across a crowded room, and the ceiling of the universe came hailing down. Maybe it's true, because the two of them have been veritable Siamese Twins ever since. The Stilletto backing band included Fred Smith (who has since worked with Television and the current Richard Lloyd Band as well as Blondie) and drummer Billy O'Conner, both of whom followed Chris and Debbie off on their sojourn in search of the Higher Truth and *Midnight Special* guest-host slots. From the first night Emerson brought him over, Chris started hanging around, and though the precise chronology is a little vague he was playing guitar in the band in record time and hooked up with Debbie just about as fast. But apparently there was some sort of musical as well as physical-romantic chemistry between Chris and Debbie right away, because the Stillettoes broke up almost as soon as he entered the picture.

For the next year or so, Fred, Billy, Debbie and Chris fumbled around as Angel and the Snakes, while Debbie worked as a barmaid. Anya Phillips, another friend of the Blondies, who now manages James Chance's Contortions, remembers this period well: "I first met Chris and Debbie in 1974, I'd say about August. I'd come to New York, and my first job was working as a barmaid down on Wall Street, at a place called White's Pub. It was newly opened, like the second week, and there was a girl named Jackie who was working there. She was friends with Debbie, in fact she was singing backup. This was after Stilletto and before Blondie. I guess Debbie needed a job so Jackie brought her down there to White's Pub, and that's how we met. I started going to Club 82 because that's where I'd met Jackie, and Debbie was inviting me to CBGB's to see her band. At that time there would be maybe five people in the place. I don't think they even had a cover or admission at the door yet. It was really, really empty. The Ramones opened for Angel and the Snakes. Before Jackie was singing in the band, they were going through a transition; they knew they were changing the name to Blondie and adding two girl backup singers. Tish and Snooky were in it later; this was before them. This was August, September '74, still pretty much the heavy tail end of glitter.

"Debbie wore turquoise blue stretch leotard tops and red stockings, and she used to do this song called 'Platinum Blonde,' where she had this ratty wig and this sort of beat-up dress; she'd come onstage and start singing 'I wanna be a platinum blonde,' and rip off the wig and platinum dress. Chris used to come to the pub to pick her up after work every day. He had long hair and blue eyeshadow and used to wear these leather chaps."

"Was he already pretty protective of her?" I wondered.

"Oh, very. But they hadn't been really going together all that long, I think just a few months at that point, but they were really in love, as they still are. By around October or November Jackie was singing in the band with another girl named Julie, and all three of them were blonde, so I guess that was the idea of Blondie."

"Who was writing most of the material?"

"Well, I assume it was Debbie and Chris. Chris was the leader of the band, more or less. It was pretty much the same as it is now; they were together in that they were the front people in the band. The first time I saw them I remember that Debbie was the front girl and Chris was more obtuse than the rest of the band. He was dramatic—Chris was quite flashy in those days."

"Do you have any idea why he became less flashy?"

"Not just Blondie, everybody did: six inch tiger platform shoes and stuff. Julie left New York and Jackie was not real reliable, and eventually she dropped out of the scene. The band had already been changed to Blondie. The end of '74, I'd already quit working at White's Pub but Debbie was still there, and so was Blondie.

Tish and Snooky were in the band then. Back in those days, it was still a relatively small clique, everybody just sorta went to see each other in their friends' bands."

"What were your impressions of Debbie personally? Do you still see her now?"

"Yeah. Since the first time I met her I just thought she was really, really beautiful and really, really nice, and I couldn't believe that anyone who was so beautiful could be so nice. Usually girls who are that beautiful tend to be real bitchy; they know how much power they have by their looks and they're really snotty about it, but Debbie's never been like that. Even through all her success she hasn't changed really; she's a little more harried, but she and Chris have always remained friends of mine."

In Which Yet Another Pompous Blowhard Purports to Possess the True Meaning of **Punk Rock**

bviously what was going on here was the earliest germinal stage of the late-Seventies American punk rock scene, which eventually exploded in three places: New York, London and the international communications media. But punk rock was hardly invented by the Ramones in Queens, N.Y. in 1974-5, any more than it was by the Sex Pistols in London a year or so later. You have to go back to the New York Dolls.

The truth is that punk rock is a phrase that has been around at least since the beginning of the Seventies, and what it at bottom means is rock 'n' roll in its most basic, primitive form. In other words, punk rock has existed throughout the history of rock 'n' roll, they just didn't call it that. In the Fifties, when rock 'n' roll was so new it scared the shit out of parents and racists everywhere, the media had a field day.

This stuff was derided mercilessly, it was called "unmusical," it was blamed for juvenile delinquency, sexual depravity (well . . .) if not the demise of Western civilization as a whole. It was said that the musicians could not play their instruments; in large part, by any conventional standards (what they used to call "good" music), this was true. Does that matter now to the people who are still listening to those classic oldies twenty years later? It was said that the singers could not sing, by any previous "legitimate" musical standard; this was also true. It was written off nearly everywhere as a load of garbage that would come and go within a year's time, a fad like the hula hoop.

Is any of this beginning to sound vaguely familiar?

The point is that rock 'n' roll, as I see it, is the ultimate populist art form, democracy in action, because it's true: anybody *can* do it. Learn three chords on a guitar and you've got it. Don't worry whether you can "sing" or not. Can Neil Young "sing"? Lou Reed? Bob Dylan? A lot of people can't stand to listen to Van Morrison, one of the finest poets *and* singers in the history of popular music, because of the sound of his voice. But this is simply a matter of exposure. For performing rock 'n' roll, or punk rock, or call it any damn thing you please, there's only one thing you need: NERVE. Rock 'n' roll is an *attitude*, and if you've got the attitude you can do it, no matter what anybody says. Believing that is one of the things punk rock is about. Rock is for everybody, it should be so implicitly anti-elitist that the question of whether somebody's qualified to perform it should never even arise.

But it did. In the Sixties, of course. And maybe this was one reason why the Sixties may not have been so all-fired great as we gave them credit for. Because in the Sixties rock 'n' roll began to think of itself as an "artform." Rock 'n' roll is not an "artform"; rock 'n' roll is a raw wail from the bottom of the guts. And like I said, whatever anybody ever called it, punk rock has been around from the beginning—it's just rock honed down to its rawest elements, simple playing with a lot of power and vocalists who may not have much range but have so much conviction and passion it makes up for it ten times over. Because PASSION IS WHAT IT'S ALL ABOUT— what *all* music is about.

In the early Sixties there was punk rock: "Louie, Louie" by the Kingsmen

being probably the most prominent example, it was crude, it was rude, anybody could play it but so what? It'll be around and people everywhere will still be playing it as long as there's a rock 'n' roll left at all. It's already lasted longer than *Sgt. Pepper*! Who in the hell does any songs from that album anymore? Yet, a few years ago, some people were saying *Sgt Pepper* will endure a hundred years.

Seventies punk largely reflects a reaction against the cult of the guitar hero. Technical virtuosity was not a *sine qua non* of rock 'n' roll in the first place and never should have become. Not that brilliant rock hasn't been made by musicians whose technical chops were and are the absolute highest. But see, that's JUST THE POINT. Just because something is simpler than something else does not make it worse. It's

just the kind of hype a lot of people started buying in the late Sixties with the rise of the superstar and superinstrumentalist concepts.

There was punk rock all through the Sixties. The Seeds with "Pushin' Too Hard." Count Five "Psychotic Reaction." "Talk Talk" by the Music Machine. And many others. It was simple, primitive, direct, honest music. Then, in 1969, Iggy and the Stooges put out their first album. Throughout the Seventies, that and their subsequent two albums became cult items with small groups of people all over the world, who thought these records were some of the greatest stuff they had ever heard. They were also some of the simplest: two chords, a blaring fuzztone, Iggy singing lyrics as simple as "Can ah cum ovah to-nat? Can ah cum ovah to-nat? Uh said uh we will have a real cool taam—

to-*naaat*! We will hayuv—a reeal coool taam! To-*naat*!" Get it? It was, as Ed Ward wrote in *Rolling Stone* when it appeared, "A *reductio ad absurdum* of rock 'n' roll that might have been thought up by a mad DAR general in a wet dream." Except where he was being sarcastic, I thought that was a compliment: the Stooges music was brutal, mindless, primitive, vicious, base, savage, primal, hate-filled, grungy, violent, terrifying and above all REAL. They meant every note and word of it.

Enter the Dolls. They might have taken some cues from the Stooges, but who they really wanted to be was an American garage band Rolling Stones. And that's exactly what they were. Everything about them was pure outrage. And too live for the time—'72-3-4 mostly. They set New York on fire, but the rest of the country wasn't ready for it.

I was talking to a guitarist friend, and the subject of the Dolls came up.

"God," she said, "the first time they were on TV, we just couldn't believe it, that anybody that shitty would be allowed to do that! How did they get away with it?"

I felt like throwing her out of my house. They didn't "get away" with anything. They did what they could and what they wanted to do and out of the chaos emerged something magnificent, something that was so literally explosive with energy and life and joy and madness that it could not be held down by all your RULES of how this is supposed to be done! Because none of 'em are valid! Rock 'n' roll is about BREAKING the form, not "working within it." GIVE US SOME EQUAL TIME. Let the kid behind the wheel. Like Joe Strummer of the Clash says, "It's not about playin' the chords right, for starters!"

And in the summer of 1976, the Ramones did their first tour of England. Kids all over that nation went crazy. They saw how easy the music was to play, how exciting it was, how much fun, and they went out and got instruments and did it. *Voilà*—Sex Pistols. Clash. And the faceless ten million that followed.

So back to the narrative we broke off for history, righteous truths and contextual background, which will come in handy later when we start hearing people complain about how Blondie themselves "can't play." Blondie always differed from many, perhaps most others issuing up from CBGB's, in that they were inspired not so much by the Stooges as by mainstream mid-Sixties pop *à la* Beatles, with Phil Spector ahead by a furlong. And the

Blondies' refangled regurgitation of old BeatlesSpectorShangri-La'sTurtlesBeach Boys *et al* riffs would almost out of necessity have to be served up with a heavy topping—or is it core—of camp-Warholvian irony, ambivalence, emotional inside-out blackout hijinx.

Around CBGB's in those days it was the Ramones, the Heartbreakers featuring Johnny Thunders (ex-New York Dolls) and Richard Hell (ex-Television), as well as Television itself, Talking Heads, the Miamis, a couple of other groups, and Blondie.

So, Chris and Debbie and Fred Smith and drumbug Billy O'Conner were slithering by in thriftshop raiment as Angel and the Snakes, verging on into the first christened moments of Blondie, late-'74-early-'75.

Miami Jimmy Wyndbrandt picks up the thread: "So Chris and Debbie were downtown now living on Thompson Street, trying to get a band together, and Fred Smith wound up as the bass player, with Billy O'Conner on drums. Meanwhile Chris and Debbie had the only car of anybody I knew in town, and could always be counted on if there was a real pinch with anything to help out with their car. It was a real grind, they were struggling to get their thing together, but the band was very untogether usually. I think Chris was the only guitar player."

Correct.

"So it was like a trio with Debbie, Chris, the other two, and then they used Tish and Snooky for a while. It didn't work out; I think Debbie figured they weren't helping further the group image, it just wasn't right for what they were doing."

Tish and Snooky Bellomo should need no introduction but for the time being, still do. These sisters have more innate spontaneous style in their pinkies than most people got in their lumbering corpuses. Since mid-summer-'77 they've been running a punk boutique called Manic Panic in New York, which is the only such store in this whole town founded and forging ahead in the absolute spirit which birthed this music in the first place.

Tish and Snooky have personality to burn, and what's more can really sing. Debbie knew a good thing when she saw it, and hired them.

Here they take up the story, after I was ignorant enough to ask "I guess you guys kinda came in when Elda went out, eh?"

Tish: "There was a space in between where they played around a bit as Angel and the Snakes. She saw us sing in this show called the Palm Casino Review at the Bowery Lane Theatre across from CBGB's."

"Yeah," laughs Snooky, "we started out in vaudeville."

Tish continues: "And we used to run across the street between sets. I think Gorilla Rose introduced us; he was in the Palm Casino Review and he used to be in these shows at CBGB's with Tomata du Plenty, who later was in the Screamers out in L.A. Sorta camp Theatre of the Ridiculous type stuff. So he introduced us to Debbie and Chris, because Tomata and Gorilla were friends with them, and they said they needed two backups. We just sorta fell into it, and it was real simple stuff."

"Were they doing a sort of camp glitter thing," I asked, "or already starting to sound like they do now?"

"It was a mixture of camp and at one point they decided to be like a Top 40 cover band, they would do things like 'Lady Marmelade.'"

"Can you describe some of the costumes?"

"Everybody sort of wore whatever they

BRIDES OF THE PUNK APOCALYPSE: SNOOKY (L) AND TISH (R)

wanted to wear, and wore different things; like me 'n' Snooky used to wear go-go dresses a lot, and miniskirts. Debbie would wear stretch pants; she didn't care for skirts that much. Gorilla used to call us Tish and Snooky à Go Go. But it became officially called Blondie and the Banzai Babies. I think it was Chris' idea. It was the late summer of '74 when we started. We were playing at Performance Studios, this place where everybody used to rehearse: the Ramones, Blondie, Tuff Darts. It was just this tiny little place off Broadway on 20th St."

"So what was your stage show like?"

"Well, it was usually Debbie on one side and me and Snooky on the other side, and at one point they wanted one of us to be on each side of her, because they thought we

TISH AND SNOOKY IN THE SIC FUX: THE BRONX COULD DO WORSE.

Stillettoes ↑
Club 82 / June '74

Debbie in
"Union City" ↴

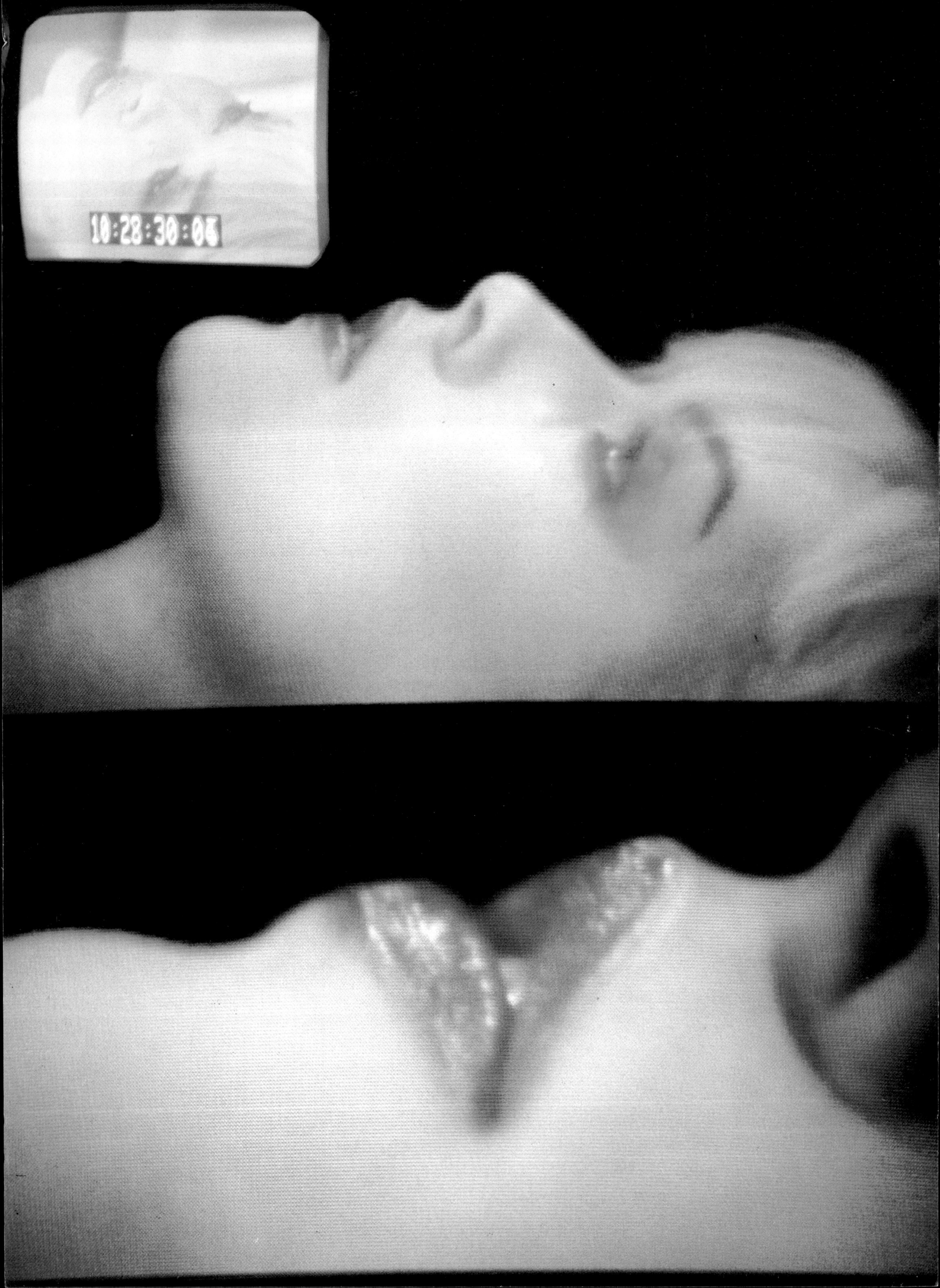
10:28:30:06

almost like 'We gotta do a few of Jimmy's songs, a few of our songs …' I think what was going on then was the band was trying to assert itself, and Debbie was trying with a conscious effort not to make it the blonde bombshell, and they did, but ….

"Clem has turned out to be probably one of the top five drummers in rock 'n' roll today. He's remarkable, and Jimmy has grown up, Chris' guitar playing has really improved, and the two new guys that I didn't have the opportunity to work with, the bass player and guitar player, they were just experimenting with them on the second album. They've really added a lot to the group since then. And 'Denis,' I keep going back to it, but the humor and fun in there were just, well … with a Jersey accent to start singing in French was … just really fabulous. Hell, I wanted 'em to do 'Heart of Glass,' but they never wanted to do it. Actually it wasn't called 'Heart of Glass' yet, it was still just their 'disco song,' but it was essentially the same record, melody, lyrics. But they just never wanted to do it."

"Because it was disco music?"

"Could be. I think a lot of the material on *Eat to the Beat* is new, on *Parallel Lines* there were a lot of songs they had from before, and that they've still got a lot of great early things that they've never done."

Chris was not entirely happy with the second album, either, and as for the lyrics, well … I said to him, "Most of the people I know don't understand what a lot of your songs are about. I'd be the first to admit that I'm one of them."

"Well," he said, "lyrically a lot of the songs go fairly deep into various things. We had that one song, 'Sniper,' that was one I wrote about a kid shooting cars that was prophetic actually in terms of heralding the coming trends. That was right before Son of Sam. And 'I'm on E' is about the gas shortage, that came out long before that was goin' on."

"Oh, yeah? 'Cause I asked Gottehrer about that and—"

"'E' means empty."

"Yeah, I caught that when you just said it, but he said he thought it was more 'I'm on open E tuning, I'm blanked out, wiped out,' and he said he didn't understand a lot of the lyrics on the album as a whole."

"We had a lot of problems making that album, because that was right when Gary left."

"Well, then, would you say that the album was somewhat misconceived?"

"Ah, there was just like no real conception. And then also I believe in the second album syndrome, where a band will have this outpouring of fresh energy on their first album, and then especially in the New Wave all the second albums were disappointing initially: look at Television, Patti, the Ramones …"

"I wasn't disappointed in Television or the Ramones' second albums myself. And I thought Talking Heads' second was *better* than their first."

"Well, a lot of people were. Especially critics. But I just think that's a syndrome. For one thing, the songs we had on the first album were all played for years and years, and that stuff on the second album, only one, 'Love at the Pier,' was an old song. The rest of 'em were done for the album."

Since they had enjoyed such a string of hit singles all over the rest of the world before "Glass" cracked America—you'll hear people comparing them to Abba, though I don't think that fits at all—I asked him how he and the group had felt about being chartbusters everywhere but their home turf.

"The way the singles have been handled in America, from Private Stock on, has not been too hot. I think we have consistently had the wrong singles released on us. They did release 'Denis' here but it didn't do anything because that was when Southern rock was still dominating everything. The lyric was partially in French and everything, but the bottom line is it was power pop and nobody was ready for it. Whereas at the same time it was a massive hit all over Europe; it was Number One in those countries for months."

"Well, didn't you say in one interview that the group is kind of a European group?"

"Well, yeah, we've always had a European appeal; in the European press with Jimmy's Farfisa and all we've always had an Italian bar band image."

I don't ask him whether he thinks that's funny. I figure he could laugh for himself if he felt like it.

In an interview in the December 1979 issue of *Record Review* magazine, new guitarist and bassist Frank Infante (who played a bit on *Plastic Letters*) and Nigel Harrison (who didn't) were asked roughly the same question, and Frank said, "I think we played in Europe more than we played here. There's a lot more territory to cover here. It's not easy to become a success in England, but compared to America, I think it's a lot easier."

"There's one TV show," explained Nigel, who's British himself, *"Top of the Pops*, and if you get a halfway decent record [in England] you're guaranteed a lot of sales. If it's a good record, you're guaranteed a Top Ten."

But surely it can't be that simple. Probably the key lies in the simple realization that, as in so many other areas, America no longer leads the world musically. Though really for generations it's almost been something of a tradition how many of our best cultural products are disregarded or disliked at home, found open arms in Europe, and sometimes decades later, maybe finally found their just rewards back here. There's no reason why it should be any different for the Blondies, especially since, with so much of their material, they don't especially make it easy on themselves or the casual or even uncasual listener anyway.

It would seem that Blondie have always wanted to consider themselves at least capable of dipping into the avant-garde. Chris has expressed his admiration of Andy Warhol on more than one occasion. They were never all that far from Soho in temperament whatever the geography; and despite the fact that you may think some of these manifestations a little pretentious, they received what probably amounted to certified seal of approval and welcome to The Club when, one night in the summer of 1978, Robert Fripp, guitar experimentalist, sat in on a Blondie gig at CBGB's and they did Donna Summer's "I Feel Love."

It got a lot of press, and I wouldn't be at all surprised if it was this which finally led them to cut "Heart of Glass," though given the aforestated closeness to the arty/fashion/conceptualist sphere that Chris and Debbie (if no one else in the band) maintained from the beginning, it was no surprise. And it certainly should not have been misconstrued as some "sellout to disco," since disco's what they play, as everybody knows, at all them places like Studio 54, where after "Glass'" success The Warhol itself threw a party for Debbie. According to the *New York Times*, she was recognized by few of the patrons over 25 even though she had known Warhol for years and her face was gracing the cover of his *Interview* rag that very month. She ended up trying to escape from her own party and almost not being able to, picked clean as the cousin in *Suddenly, Last Summer* by a whirring swarm of *paparazzi*.

It's so hard to tell the avant-garde from Bloomingdale's anymore that maybe it's best just not to even ask. Fripp, not long after their jam-nite, did ask Debbie to sing the Summer song on *Exposure*, the solo album he was then preparing for Polydor. But, in a move that one supposes is typical of record company theories on How To Build Promising Artists Into Hot Property Superstars, Chrysalis replied with a flat *No*, explaining, according to Fripp, that "Deborah Harry has a voice in a million." Well, so does Jody Maxwell of *Screw*, so what? Fortunately for Blondie and their fans, Fripp was a gentleman and adult enough not to retaliate, and contributed some rippling guitar figures to *Parallel Lines'* "Fade Away and Radiate."

While all of this was going on, new hard-rock bedrock was laid into the band in the form of Frank Infante (guitar) and Nigel Harrison (bass).

Nigel is a veteran of Michael Des-Barres glitter albatross Silverhead, of *16 and Savaged* demisemisometimefame. After that he did a little relatively painless time in Ray Manzarek's (ex-Doors) Nite City. He doesn't have the 3-D sharp personality of Valentine, but he fits.

Frank's a Jersey City boy who'd previously played with a whole lot of bands, probably better off left uncited, on one of the grungiest circuits in America. But he has proven to be positive *ballast* owing not only to his only-Jersey-natural rockchops but to how they can offset some of Chris' Twinkie Zone tendencies.

"Our styles are different," Frank told *Record Review*. "Chris is more into electronic sounds and I'm more into just getting down and playing the guitar. I played on 'One Way or Another,' that's more my style."

FRANK AND NIGEL GET HAPPY.

Chapman. With a smile on his face. Because he knows that HE is on the radio, blaring in any dashboard, that sound, that one precise peculiar never quite isolatable sound, well, Mike Chapman owns it.

"If you can't make hit singles," Chapman told *Rolling Stone*'s Jamie James in Chris Stein's favorite article, "you should fuck off and go chop meat somewhere."

So long, Leonard Cohen, nice knowin' ya I guess.

Chapman had been a Blondie aficionado from afar since their first album. "I love their first LP," he told *New York Rocker*, "the arrangements and ideas were great, but it was badly put together." He added that *Parallel Lines* "was a hard album to make because nobody was used to the discipline I require when I make an album. In the past they'd record and it'd be, 'I guess that's okay.' It took lots of energy to get the tracks down and make them better than okay. I'm glad I did it."

Yes and so are elevators the world over.

I don't know if *Parallel Lines* is New Wave for that great mythic Ozzie and Harriet audience out there in the heartland (somehow I doubt it), but I do know what Mike means when he says that unlike its predecessors this album was "polished, tight and varied"; he also hit the nail square on the head re Chris' artsy pretences and the band's general worth in the broader scheme of things by adding "It's good light listening—that's what Blondie's all about."

Okay. And, uh, make it on toast please, whole wheat.

On the question of punk rock, Chapman has this to say to one interviewer: "I didn't make a punk album or a New Wave album with Blondie. I made a pop album. If the radio stations would only forget this evil word 'punk-rock.' It's modern rock 'n' roll. Punk-rock doesn't exist or it does in England but they're so far behind the rest of the world that it doesn't really matter."

Guess that takes care of that.

Except there is a contradiction between Chapman's "light" listening and what people have called Debbie's unemotional singing and zombielike stage presence. There is a coldness about the whole band that becomes more emphatic each time they put out a new album. Almost none of them ever smiles in publicity shots, as if to

say, "Don't underestimate us, folks. This isn't just some pop fluff, we are Serious People with Important Things To Say."

So let's say that Blondie aren't just a fun, pop group, making "good light listening." Let's say there's a real art statement being made here. Try to figure out through all the obfuscations exactly what it is.

Of course we'll use *Parallel Lines*, because that is the album in which they got their big Statement out to the most people so far. The record's practically a household word by now, so if there is potential for political revolution in *this* group, *this* album has spread the clear light of the vision farthest.

Perhaps it's Blondie's image as Good Clean Wholesome Rock 'n' Roll Kids Who Made It Big as much as the music that keeps *Parallel Lines* swimming around the antipodes of the charts, never quite dropping off. People seem to just keep buying and buying it, like *Rumours* or something equally ineluctable.

I still refuse to believe that any of the songs on this album are about anything. The general gist of many of Blondie's lyrics and perhaps their whole stance might be summed up in the lyrics from an unfinished song by Deborah after which the album was named. They're printed on the inner sleeve, and they probably make more sense as a poem anyway; aside from some babble about someone named Evangeline, the idea seems to be that whether we're talking about the song, the printed page, the mosaic blear that comes off the external coaxial umbilical, or you and me, there is no reconciliation possible: "It's parallel lines that will never meet."

"Parallel Lines": Zero Cool

his *Philosophy*, Nothing is always tasteful, always in style, always discreet.

As for Debbie, she's letting us know that just because there are words all over this lyric sheet doesn't mean they have to follow like literature or "Mr. Tambourine Man" or even "Sugar Sugar." The words can stand on their own, each one separate and complete unto itself, an *objet d'art* suspended in the space between your headphone ears. It has long been established that the vast majority of pop record buyers and rock fans never listen to lyrics anyway, unless they've got dirty ones stuck in there somewhere. There are just entities, countless billions of them, all of absolutely equivalent significance and value.

The Blondies are hip to Post-Modernism, and Post-Modernism is hip to them, which is why even their most bland-out lyrics get quoted in *Village Voice* articles on the subject. It's a marriage of convenience. And convenience is the name of the game, otherwise why bother with anything? Make it spare and clean and fast. Above all, don't expect. Because it isn't there. I'm not there. I say what I mean: Nothing. Cathode trance is perfect orgone isolation, fixed beyond Burroughs, goes on long as Con Ed holds out. But the lines are fixed, too. No cheap sentiment or jackoff rage: passion in this context is useless as a luxury liner in the middle of the Sahara. As for the reference to Evangeline, I seriously doubt that it has anything to do with any heroine of any poem by Longfellow. Evangeline is just another word, a unit in the mosaic blear at the end of the coaxial cable or the trail of type and don't fall over the edge. But these people are beyond injokes, beyond coy, beyond their own beyondness. Nada chucks Dada out the window, byebye clutter.

The thing that makes *Parallel Lines* assuredly avant-garde is precisely that it's so airtight and multiple-varnished, such a pristinely slick piece of product it's not even vapid like Barry Manilow, who at least can embarrass/make you throw up

In other words, as John Lydon (ex-Johnny Rotten) said in a far different universe, "Words are useless/I see it in your eyes." That you got no eyes. In other words, no words. The meaning of all of this may be measured inversely to its secular/practical/spiritual application, and the most profoundly meaningful thing—in fact the only meaningful thing left in the entire universe is—nothing. Beautiful Nothing. The Warhol, Deb's Unca Andy himself couldn'ta put it better. Like he said in

once in awhile with an "At the Copa." Nope. This is it. The masterpiece. Gotta be, because its dimensions are so perfect: no bottom, no top, no sides, no rides, no new nows no how. Each song is a perfectly constructed concave system in which every single piece of information offered up in the lyrics cancels out another corresponding piece of information, kinda like a jigsaw puzzle except at the end instead of a picture you get a perfect blank. And that blank of course is nothing less than Deborah Harry's face.

I used to think a lot of Blondie's more recent songs were about emotional ambivalence—now I know that's investing them with far too much tragic weight. They'd collapse under the strain. When Debbie sings she's gonna *getcha getcha gitcha!* it's obvious that she doesn't mean that she's gonna appropriate your bod for the carnal or your soul to quench the pangs of love she's always made a point of not having. A friend of mine said "Jesus, it's so unsensuous, it sounds like a *threat!*"

"Hanging on the Telephone" has more to do with romance with the receiver, wires, telephone mechanism and attendant technology itself than any human "relationship." She's hanging on that damn phone not because she likes the sounds of your voice or cares about what you're saying, *but because she feels comforted by the bare fact 'n' act of holding it in her hand.* Anybody or indeed anything could be on the other end, you're replaceable and don't ever dare forget it or it might be your last mistake in this life. Health may be measured by degrees of stasis. Except all the yardsticks have been used for kindling —oh well. One of us is here. A photo would do as well.

"Fade Away and Radiate," is a companion piece in a way to "Hanging on the Telephone," another love song to a piece of technical furniture with the only true life force, the one that comes not from the womb but the wall, humming through it. No wonder Chris and Debbie's relationship has held together so long in a time when people can't seem to connect: they're like Ralf and Florian with one sex change between the two (You first, my dear Alphonse ...), sitting up next to each other in bed, each making love with totally skilled concentration to the electronic gadget of his or her choice. Occasionally a hand reaches around the back, meets another, they squeeze briefly, contact made, base touched, and pull away, back to the real reel deal, the empty floursack heart's last whispered wish, to keep *on* that little bugger tapping out those codes in combinations and permutations infinite as Borges' Library of Babylon until you hit that PERFECT CONNECTION where everything merges and nothing needs 'cause you won't exist.

I know Deborah's game. She, like Chris, has been to Andy-School, and sometimes I think she may have learned her lessons far better than he. Like for instance that the hottest market-valued commodity you can give 'em now is an undifferentiated screen, a field upon which they can project themselves, whatever it is they want to see or think they want to see or think they do see when they don't because there's nothing there and their pupils were clouded over through disuse a while back and they didn't even notice it but that's okay just like everything else. I know but I don't know. That's what I call a feeling of *completion*. No schizophrenia here—just two perfectly symbiotic interlocking yinyang halves!

"11:59" is almost too urgent for this album, till you realize that for Jimmy or the protagonist in this song it's gonna be 11:59 forever. When the Ramones called their last album *End of the Century*, they were automatically implying the beginning of something new, gotta have some action, why sit around 30 years waiting for a castle to fall outa the air when we can blast through on methedrine time and FIND OUT. This of course is the antithesis, or obverse, the only thing could kill it'd be the stroke of twelve. Will anything happen? The question's already answered itself.

"Sunday Girl" is like Sunday afternoon TV. Either that or the closeness of the Other is only bearable because of this context of utter becalmitude, the motionless air of the day of rest. Song's about a pillow, not a girl.

"Just Go Away" is a nice way to close an album that never opened to begin with, kind of like a locked, barred and bolted door marked PRIVATE, not overkill but dry humor perhaps, pre-fab as you, just add water but not while I'm around please, I can't stand the sight of living growing organic things.

"**H**eart of Glass." Never saw the Herzog movie. Nick Tosches told Debbie when he interviewed her for *Creem*, "There's no such movie." Probably not. Is there such a group as Blondie? What difference does it make? You and they have no particular reason to be physically around each other. And even if there are six human beings somewhere who have devoted their lives to the maintenance of a rock group with this name, they still haven't come up with anything within leagues of "Sugar Sugar," which means they could never be as real or heavy as the Archies who never ever existed.

Probably the slight palpable but bearable tickly tension of that eternally unfulfilled promise as disco's rhythms are unreleased was what made this song such a blanket hit for so long in every bar—every restaurant-disco-punk club-old folks' home-hospital-prison. It curled through the wires, drifting out and down the air like a fume of soma. Putting to well-earned rest burning hearts and nerves. A heart of glass might be ultimately vulnerable, but you didn't necessarily see the vault and armored car up there, the driver motionless and the subject of "The Hardest Part." All your acetylene in the world will never get it open. You don't want it open.

And the alternatives are so much more interesting: disco: an airlock. Blondie: a nonentity and five apathetic young fellows. They're nobodies, she's a nonentity, there's a difference. They exist. Tough luck.

And how did the Blank Generation receive this ultimate paean to its stance and aims? With incomprehension and hostility, as usual. Certainly it's much closer to the, well, heart of all those things than Richard Hell's song was. But people are getting more Pavlovian all the time, and there's all kinds of them walking around with little buzzers in their heads that whenever they hear the word "disco" or a certain type of beat or even a rhythm box the alarm's tripped and it's riot in the cell block again.

For Blondie, of course, "Heart of Glass" was the breakthrough they'd been working towards all along (I think): it went Number One all across these United States, possibly the only thing they were united upon that week. Chris just shrugged the whole thing off. "We didn't expect the song to be that big," he told *Circus* magazine for a pseudo rabble-rousing article entitled "Why Are Rockers Going Disco?" "We did it as a novelty item to put more diversity into the album. We thought 'Picture This' and 'Pretty Baby' would be big hits in the States. Naturally, we were proven wrong ... I suppose we should be concerned with the disappointment of our fans. But if they're that strict that they'll get concerned because we do a song like 'Heart of Glass,' I can't have much sympathy for them. It's not selling out. It's only one song."

"Eat to the Beat": A PF Flyer Sandwich (Hold the Mayo)

In *Stargazer*, his brilliant study of the Warhol world of the Sixties, Stephen Koch described Warhol as "one whose presence is defined as an absence." In this sense, then, Blondie's most pressing problem post-"Heart of Glass" would be how in the world to follow up so perfect a white hole as *Parallel Lines?*

Eat to the Beat is not really the answer, possibly because there is no answer to such a question, but it's neither failure nor water-treading either. What it is is about a fifty-fifty proposition: fifty percent songs that stand on their own as fine pieces of pop rock without the necessity of some philosophical or techno-theocratic system behind the proceedings; fifty percent dross and failed experiments and songs that for one reason or another—like, crankiness, say—turn the listener off in spite of fine craftsmanship. There's no "Heart of Glass" here, of course—"Dreaming," although a great song and a fine single, didn't come close.

In many ways this is more an *album*-album than the other three: it's hard to think of very many cuts which resemble likely hit singles, anywhere in the world.

DEBBIE WITH FANS: THIS WAS THE NOBLEST JERSEYITE OF THEM ALL.

day in the life of an industrial worker, or just a sketch with no real action or resolution I've never been able to fully work out. "Dreaming" is about emotional distance again: "Dreaming is free," and a great piece of pop craftsmanship on every level.

"Union City Blue," reportedly written by Debbie during a break on the set of, but not featured in the movie of the same title in which she was starred, has a dreamy, melancholy feeling that suggests wasted lives, a sense of mystery inside the drabness of day-to-day Middle American life that comes through like a gust of wind, and "Shayla" works somewhat similar ground to even stronger effect. Loosely patterned on a lot of Archetypal Rock Classics of the past—"Crimson and Clover," lots of girl group songs—it tells another slight but effective story, with supernatural (or extraterrestrial) overtones this time. As near as I've made out, it's about an isolated, unhappy woman who goes for a drive on the freeway, where in the last second before losing her life in a collision she perceives... Something, out there, something mystical and complete and redemptive, either flying saucers or some universal Force. It's left deliberately vague and open to various interpretations.

The thing that strikes me about "Dreaming," "Union City Blue," and "Shayla," is that all of them, and especially the last two, are a lot closer to real, achingly human passions than almost anything they've recorded since the first album, perhaps more deeply felt than anything they've ever recorded before. So much of Blondie's music is intentionally anti-emotional that one may find oneself unduly grateful for the slightest scraps of passion, yearning, empathy, anything. But all three of those qualities are definitely in "Shayla" and "Union City Blue." Debbie has, in certain interviews, expressed an identification with the mainstream working people of America not unlike Bruce Springsteen's in its root honesty and lack of condescension—as she said, she's been a "waitress in a donut shop" too. Maybe these songs are the result.

"Accidents Never Happen" is a fairly traditional and straightforward uptempo rock love song with wry quasi-mystical overtones not unlike "I Can See For Miles." Now if Debbie would only sing it with a tenth of the soaring passion Daltrey mustered back there; it's not that she turns in a bad job, she does everything she's supposed to in all the right places, but, to me, still just sounds ... *indifferent*.

And that's no putdown—the best ones work fine in context, besides which I wouldn't be surprised to find the selection I'd've thought unlikeliest of all becoming a hit, because I've been wrong so many times before, never would have predicted most of their past hits just from listening to them on the albums.

"Dreaming" only got as far as the Top Twenty, so as of this writing they're trying for "The Hardest Part," which seems dubious except for the hook of the sex joke in the lyrics, which could carry it over into almost novelty status, the kind of thing people listen to again and again to make sure they get all the words and haven't missed any smut. "The Hardest Part" also seems to contain at least the lineaments of a story, but whether it's the story of a robbery, a drab

On the Merits of Sexual Repression

Maybe this gets down to it: the Ronettes, the Shangri-La's, the Crystals, the guy singers too, all those old classic rock 'n' roll songs were fueled by one thing: *sexual repression*, and consequent frustration. They may have been sexist, they may have been neurotic or even masochistic—sometimes I think the whole reason pop music was invented in the first place was to vent sick emotions in a deceptively lulling form. THEY WERE LITERALLY EXPLOSIVE WITH ALL THAT PENT-UP LUST AND FEAR AND GUILT AND DREAD AND HATE AND RESENTMENT AND CONFUSION. And it gave them a kind of anarchic power, which can still move us.

Listening to certain old Shangri-La's sides, you might find yourself laughing and crying at the same time. And the Spector stuff ... not just the storied Wall of Sound but the *urgency* in those girl's voices spelled pure sex, distillate of every scene between a boy and girl at the drive-in, vacant lots, house when the folks were out, wherever we found to sneak off to back then to see how far we could take it this time.

All that frustration got channeled into rock, all those powerful emotions were way out front and there was plenty of meticulous detail in the productions behind them. They were like magnificent tapestries depicting the most embarrassing and ridiculous yet painful situations, and they stand to this day.

While Blondie hardly constitutes a Wall of Sound, it wouldn't be fair to hold that against them. They're not the Blondie Orchestra, they're a good little rock 'n' roll band which has been steadily evolving from the garage without ever losing sight and understanding of what was good, if not better than the rest, back there. Their songs are mostly good. Debbie's got about as good a voice by traditional "singing" standards as a lot of the people who recorded in the early Sixties. But you wouldn't dare line one of these cuts up next to a Spector or Shangri-La's production, because it'd sound downright pallid. The

reason you wouldn't is that (as I keep harping on) the music seems to have no really strong emotions in it, and what emotions do surface occasionally, what obsessions and lusts, are invariably almost immediately gutted by fusillades of irony, sarcasm, camp, what have you, ending up buried.

IF THE MAIN REASON WE LISTEN TO MUSIC IN THE FIRST PLACE IS TO HEAR PASSION EXPRESSED—as I've believed all my life—THEN WHAT GOOD IS THIS MUSIC GOING TO PROVE TO BE? What does that say about us? What are we confirming in ourselves by doting on art that is emotionally neutral? And, simultaneously, what in ourselves might we be destroying or at least keeping down?

In the last few years we have seen the rise of a type of music perhaps previously unknown in human history: music designed specifically, by intent or subconscious motivation, to remove what emotions might linger in the atmosphere around us, creating a vacuum where we can breathe easier because we're not so freaked by each other even though we still don't communicate. That's your basic disco, of course. But it's not just disco music that does this. It's all kinds of music and you can talk all you want about muzak and the wimsy weasly pre-rock popular music our parents lived and loved to, "How Much is That Doggie in the Window," but that wasn't the same, because all those songs were based upon a view of social intercourse pretty much agreed upon by everyone listening. Whereas no such thing really exists now. So there's a whole new genre of music, it's like vacuum cleaner music, or air conditioner music, climate control, antidepressant/antipsychotic music, music designed to neutralize and pacify and ultimately render stillness rather than the jungle pounding of two lovers' hearts or the Beaver Cleaver sappiness of "Doggie in the Window." Before, all music you heard was designed to put something *into* the room; this new stuff is designed to take something *out*.

Blondie have, it seems, embraced this aesthetic more or less wholeheartedly. But when you're always taking out instead of putting in ... well, it's just like a bank account, isn't it? Pretty soon there's gonna be nothing left. And that kinda would seem to make you a musical vampire, of sorts.

Patti Smith, for all her pretensions, her wrongheadedness, her narcissism, her addled crusades, is still singing from her

however mottled heart. She contributes something to the environment when she's on, she stands for something too no matter how etc., but she's real, flesh and blood comes through those grooves, which I think is one reason why she has so many fans. Or Lou Reed, for all his monotonal mutterings, there so much pain suffused just under the monotone, so much despair and desire and human regret, that even at his most cynical you can feel him struggling with himself, fighting his demons. But Blondie ... do they have that kind of courage?

Like Bryan Ferry in Roxy Music, they're trying to create a sort of deliberately rococo, overstuffed art rock that hides what the artist is truly feeling by dropping well-turned ironies all over the place, by coming up with synthetic soul-searchings that purport to be even more interesting than the real thing. Or they just camp it up. But even Bryan Ferry was in the grips of real romantic lobster claws, and no matter how many times he transposed what he was going through before putting it out in song you always knew he was going through *something*. There was a grand passion, a vitality and even kind of poignancy about his music even at its archest and most exasperatingly evasive.

Whereas with Blondie you get no such vibe, 90% of the time at least. What you get instead is a pervasive coldness, and even that's not so bad, since they don't just write pop love songs. What are they driving at in most of their lyrics? Are they telling you to leave them alone? Are they kvetching about their career? Are they concocting little sagas based on everyday events that never become compelling? Or are they being deliberately mundane to the point of madness? .... What, if anything, do these people actually *care* about?

Or if all they want to do is entertain, then why do they act so serious about what they're doing? Maybe they think they're Dorothy Parker, commenting lightly and wittily on the passing mobs without ever getting in too deep. Which is okay, too, except .... It's impenetrable. Talk about walls of sound, THEIR MUSIC IS A WALL. It's designed that way, most likely from self-protective instincts that're not necessarily unjustified or misguided but ... they're dealing in media that ostensibly communicate ... then eventually the audience begins to receive an impression of some hermetic body of people, a little cabal,

who've locked themselves in and are nursing a siege mentality when nobody really is out to get them.

The press ain't nice, don't play fair, you get burned once and you're more careful next time. But you don't walk around in these giant suits of armor and exoskeletons steeling yourselves against new attacks every corner you turn. Sooner or later, you would have to say something you really mean. "Shayla" and "Union City Blue" come closest, but they're both third-person songs. When are Blondie gonna write a first person song—aside from "Living in the Real World," which is just an awfully early case of the old familiar syndrome of rockstar selfpity—that expresses how they truly feel about themselves, each other, their friends, lovers, acquaintances, relatives, the landlord, ANYBODY, ANYTHING. Just make it definite and act like you mean it.

To maintain stardom as a function of non-empathetic distance, to keep them wanting more even as you toss the dirt of your contempt in their faces or just turn your back like Miles Davis did for most of his career ... well, this is no easy trick to pull off. It takes an extremely complex personality and one who is also a master of shifting masks and disguises, the compleat chameleon (Dylan, Bowie). Either that or the innate ability to project something menacing and dangerous, however spurious this impression may be, that keeps them at bay (Lou Reed). Most artists of any type just don't have it.

Debbie, to me, is transparently a nice girl, not insipid like some but hardly redolent of danger. Who among our celebrity/folk-heroes *is* redolent of danger anymore? They're all a bunch of bland-outs. That seems to be what people want. Maybe, in fact, that very craving accounts for more of Blondie's popularity than we might have previously suspected.

Let it never be forgotten that until Patti Smith slashed through the barriers like a henbane banshee in 1975, rock was almost exclusively a male-supremacist world. Most of the early Sixties girl groups were too ethnic, too Eastern seaboard streetgang-vibed for the kind of mass crossover appeal Debbie's achieved. Janis Joplin was too pathetic, a freak for the freaks. Grace Slick prefers her vast storehouse of private jokes and has gone out of her way to be *un*glamorous. Patti's still too jungle for *TV Guide*. So that leaves one person, the woman whose fate it is to end up getting called the "Queen of Punk."

BLONDIE
On **PRIVATE STOCK RECORDS** and GRT Tapes

Outside Tracks, Hobbies & The Lure of Celluloid

In a sense, the Blondies can be broken down into two basic camps: Chris and Debbie, who have always been very into the Manhattan art/media/fashion scene; and the rest of the band, who are pretty much straight rockers.

"I think if they had any spare time from Blondie, Clem and Jimmy'd be jamming with somebody else in a basement somewhere," one friend put it. In spite of the demands of success, the band have made it clear that they're available whenever possible to give younger bands advice about how not to get screwed in the music biz, etc. Blondie have been very active recently in helping newer, younger talents on the New York New Wave club scene get themselves together, and it's not as if they'd "abandoned" all their "old friends" down at the usual punk watering holes to preen for the photogs at 54 every night.

I wouldn't be surprised if everybody in the group wants, sooner or later, to produce other groups. Jimmy Destri has worked with Marty Thau on an album featuring the Student Teachers, one of the younger bands on the New York club scene. Clem, just like his heroes before him, promotes Premier drums in the English press, and, inasmuch as not Ringo, Charlie Watts nor Keith Moon ever got around to producing, he might indeed be the sole Blondie to live out his life without spending some time behind the control boards.

As for Chris, he's been involved with enough outside musical projects to constitute a separate career. First was a single and album of "violin music" by Walter Steding, done for Thau's own label Red Star Records. Steding was a sort of berserko one-man band who appeared onstage with his electric violin hooked up to little electronic boxes running all round his body, whereupon he'd commence to saw away madly while punching buttons and turning dials for an effect that was a cross between the Velvet Underground's "Black Angel's Death Song" and being eaten alive by locusts.

In the winter of 1980, Chris worked on a demo tape with New York's "fake jazz" band, the Lounge Lizards, and completed production for Ze records on a group called Casino Music, two French dudes with a Stedinglike disco act. He also wrote and performed the score for *Union City*, the full-length feature film which starred Debbie.

And there was "Call Me," a Blondie number written especially for the Paul Schrader film *American Gigolo* by German disco meister Giorgio Morodor.

"Giorgio wrote the music and produced it," says Chris, "Debbie wrote the lyrics."

Chris has also been an ardent photographer for years, and has kept an extensive photo-chronologue of the band's history from inception which he plans to publish as a book.

What the whole band does like is video. A lot of people think rock video-cassettes are going to be the big thing in the years ahead. As easily as purchasing the latest album by your favorite group, you will buy a whole package—music and an album's duration of dynamite outasite wowzow visuals.

The Blondies have already been experimenting, on the tube and on their own. They are the first band in rock 'n' roll to invest in a full-length videotrack to accompany their newest album. The *Eat to the Beat* videocassette was in the stores in time for Christmas '79. With the help of producer Paul Flattery for Jon Roseman Productions (who've made shorter video promo tapes for Elvis Costello, Electric Light Orchestra, the Doobie Brothers) and director David Mallot (a veteran of mid-Sixties *Shindig*) they conceived twelve short set-pieces to correspond with the tracks on the record itself. Synced to the LP tracks there's live performance footage with Blondie dressed entirely in black and white; a sort of Dorothy-Lamour-Meets-Dr.-Alimantado effect for "Die Young Stay Pretty"; a veritable Von Stroheimian costume period mini-melodrama set to the tale of Soviet defection in "Victor"; footage of actual New Jersey docks for "Union City Blue"; and Debbie in a brunette wig for "The Hardest Part."

Chris has been working in video since he was in art school in the early Seventies, and is a regular on *Interview* magazine music columnist Glenn O'Brien's NYC late-nite cable-TV rock talk show. According to Joey Ramone, "Chris sits there talking about how to subvert the media with O'Brien and behind 'em on the wall there's a giant poster of Lenin." Pretty wild.

Probably more significant in the long run is Debbie's burgeoning movie career. Several years ago she appeared in two works by underground filmmaker Amos Poe, *Unmade Beds* (where she sang something called "Sweet Thing") and *The Foreigner* (where she sang "Old Bilbao Moon" from Kurt Weill's *The Threepenny Opera*). She was stunning-looking and competent-or-better-acting.

Poe had this to say: "Debbie's cameos are exquisite moments. She's always ready to work, very easy and fulfilling and brings something of herself to the part; she really gets into it. I think she sticks out from the rest of the film in the same way that she would stick out in a crowded room. She's not a show-off, but her presence is compelling. I believe in perfomance, it is a person's *will* that shows above all else, and that's why the critics mention her—they are *willed* to do it."

Many feature film roles for Debbie have been announced. There is supposed to be a remake of Jean-Luc Godard's *Alphaville* by Chris and Amos Poe, starring Robert Fripp and Debbie. When Debbie and Chris were on WPIX's "Radio, Radio" show in Manhattan (in Feb. 1980), a fan phoned in to ask, "Is *Alphaville* complete?"

"We just wrapped up the third version—this time it's gonna be in Panavision," replied Chris. "No, actually it's still just a glimmer of imagination."

Variety June 7, 1978 "ROCKER ON THE ROCKS," and "Choose Debbie Harry for Heavy Beat Hero Gone Ga-Ga"—"Debbie Harry, lead singer of the punk rock group Blondie, will head the cast of New Line Cinema's 'Barbie,' a rock-themed thriller to be directed by Howard Smith, Oscar winner for his feature docu *Marjoe*."

Creem magazine, December '79: "Rock 'n' Roll News"—Cheech and Chong were making a sequel to *Up in Smoke*, including Debbie in "the role of a punk rock masseuse."

People magazine, December 1979—"Movie scripts are being urged on her by both Mick Jagger and Carlo Ponti."

What *is* known to be authentically factual is that (a) the Blondies appear as themselves in *Roadie*, directed by Robert Altman protegé Alan Rudolph and starring Meat Loaf; and (b) Debbie alone completed a serious lead acting role in *Union City*, a small-budget production about lower-middle-class lives in the trenches of New Jersey. Debbie, sitting at the breakfast table drinking coffee and looking every inch the frustrated Middle American housewife in frumpy blouse and mousy brown hair was actually more striking than in the pix of her as Blondie, because the relative drabness of her dress and surroundings brought out more starkly her facial beauty.

Executive Producer Graham Belin of Kinesis Productions, the small independent company which did the picture said: "Edward Lachman, who was the director of photography, met Debbie at a party, and she said, 'I'd like to do a film sometime, and I hear you're a good photographer.' The next step was a production company, and we were chosen out of several contenders—the editing wasn't going well, so we had to make the decisions involved in getting the film into shape. Debbie and Chris were on their first U.S. tour at that time—it was after the Central Park gig in summer 1979. Anyway, we eventually pulled it into shape. It's always been visually a very beautiful film. Mark Reichert, the director, is a fine artist—as a designer of shots he's very good, but he put in a lot that wasn't necessary. We stepped in when we realized there was a very good film in there. And Chris decided to do the music.

"As for working with Debbie—she was unpretentious, she didn't lord it over us because 'Heart of Glass' had just broken. She was professional about everything, which is very unusual for major music stars. Working with her was a joy. Her abilities and potentials as an actress are both great. She needs work, but for film she's fantastic because her face is so photogenic, and she's just herself in front of the camera. You can get it on one or two takes. I think if she works with a more experienced director he'll bring her out even more. I know comparisons are odious, but I do believe she has that Marilyn Monroe quality which makes her appealing to both sexes. I don't think she took herself seriously at the beginning as an actress. She was putting herself on the line, even though everybody knew that she was a great performer.

"She would ask intelligent questions, go home and think about it and come back the next day with ideas. The only scene with her that was left out involved the frumpy housewife in her bathrobe, waking up her husband—she wanted it out. I

thought it was great—maybe she was scared she made perhaps a little too good a housewife. She looked great with spatulas in her hand.

"She *is* a housewife in a way—she cooked my partner a fish dinner, came in the next day and said, 'Well, I'm glad you're still alive.' She has a conflict, I think—one image sells and the other is where she'd like to be, I think, deep down.

"We did not want any of that *Us* magazine-type stuff going on for the film. Debbie and Chris said 'This film has nothing to do with the rock business.'

"For our film we just wanta be judged for film—we didn't exploit her, and she doesn't sing in the film. That song on the last album, 'Union City Blue,' I *think* was written when she was stuck late one night in Union City and she sat down and wrote the song to get her mind off things. But the song's not in the film. The music in the film is all instrumental, electronic oriented but it also has a piano jazz feeling to it. It's very lyrical, beautiful music, people can hear it and hum it while they're shopping … especially the opening and closing titles. Chris did a main title theme—he wrote other music, too, but when the title theme

comes out of jukeboxes and radios in cars in the film it's presented as if that was a popular song of the time.

"She's not at all like Farrah Fawcett. She does have talent. She won't sell herself like that, and if anybody else tries to do it she'll stop them. The best product today is coming from independents, and stars like Deborah Harry would rather work with them."

Interesting, I thought, *how much that resembles what happened* vis à vis *New Wave music, its reception at major record companies, and the proliferation of small independent labels.*

"I think if she has any troubles, it's because she wants to be known as Deborah Harry the actress and everyone knows her as Blondie. Her point of view is, 'Let the film speak for itself.' I don't think she would have allowed it to have gotten this far if she really hated it. She's one of the leads, but the film is not a vehicle for her. Basically she wanted to get her feet wet, and I think this was the right place and time to do it. It's a small film, and now she can go on to big things. I see it as being a good cult film, like *King of Hearts* or *Harold and Maude.*"

DEBBIE AND MINIMALIST SUITOR IN AMOS POE'S "UNMADE BEDS"

Pinups

Now we come to the inevitable, a discussion of Debbie as lust/love object. I once told Chris: "I go for the Anna Magnani type myself," and he just laughed.

People seem to have so many different kinds of weird ideas about this sex business that it's better to get things clear in front. The role that Debbie plays onstage resembles every fantasy of every badass chick I ever yearned for in high school, bad girls who followed bad boys who got them and themselves into trouble. It's a holdover image. And seems to derive from the macho notion that sexual love has to do with brutality rather than tenderness and understanding.

I remember a few years ago, I had the Big Tits poster of Debbie that Private Stock sent out with the first album up on the living room wall. I knew Debbie just like I knew most everybody else who hung around CBGB's then; we were not friends but friendly acquaintances.

And yet, *I couldn't even work up a decent pornographic fantasy about her.* I couldn't picture her with her clothes off. In fact, my lasting impression of her was of someone lost and kinda sad, a kid over 30 trapped in a role. She didn't seem to know really what she was doing on certain levels, and yet here was this poster being sent out bulk-mail so in the very moment that she's sitting there wondering just who in hell she might be, countless people from coast to coast know what her nipples look like and are cracking stupid jokes about them. What I eventually came to think of in Debbie's case was the character Carol Cutrere, in Tennessee Williams' *Orpheus Descending* (Joanne Woodward played the role in *The Fugitive Kind*, the movie version of it), this barefoot damaged innocent with matted hair all in her eyes and smudges on her cheeks, dress torn, pretending she was high and wild: "Let's go jukin'..."

While chatting over Perrier with Glenn O'Brien for *Interview* magazine one day last spring, Debbie opined that the marketing of disembodied sexual images was possibly why so many guys had turned out so screwed up:

DEBBIE: ... Do you think it's a good idea to make porno movies?

GLENN: No. I think there should be movies that are sexy or have sex in them, but I don't like pornography.

DEBBIE: Because it's dumb?

(Chris Stein enters)

CHRIS: They all suck.

GLENN: Right. All those straight busi-

ness guys, part of the reason they're the way they are is from jerking off to Playboy for twenty years.

DEBBIE: Is that what they do with them?

GLENN: Yeah, that's what they're for. Right Chris?

CHRIS: It's true. I find I myself have a fixation for photographs.

DEBBIE: I can vouch for that.

CHRIS: It's from being brought up on photographs before you can have girls. That's all it amounts to.

GLENN: But they get hooked on pictures, because they're usually of better girls than the jerker-off can get.

DEBBIE: I have a lot of twisted thoughts about it.

In *TV Guide* there's a regular ad where you can send in some money for one of those huge poster pinups of America's Golden Girls: the Angels, Cheryl, Wonder Woman, Suzanne Somers, Adrienne Barbeau—and Blondie!

There's only one hitch. It doesn't say "Deborah Harry" in the ad. It says "Blondie." Just like in *all* the ads everywhere, and all the titles of magazine stories. If it said "Deborah Harry," chances are almost nobody would send in the $2.50, because they don't know who Deborah Harry is. They just don't want to know anything about any of these women. For all of them, Deborah Harry does not exist. Which come to think of it is probably in her favor. They probably think she's some kinda Little Annie Fanny chopped 'n' channeled for the Eighties or something equally bizarre.

I know a lot of people, especially musicians, who resent Debbie and the Blondie group in general. Some cite Chris' media pretensions, but the far more universal charge is "They don't even have that much talent—they squeezed through on a cute face and some 'T. and A.'" What Debbie may not realize is that she'd end up getting hated anyway, just by being a poster girl.

I think if most guys in America could somehow get their faverave poster girl in bed and have total license to do whatever they wanted with this legendary body for one afternoon, at least 75% of the guys in the country would elect to beat her up. She may be up there all high and mighty on TV but everybody knows that underneath all that fashion plating she's just a piece of meat like the rest of them.

If Debbie Harry realizes this, though, she should never take it personally at all. It's not *her* they're enraged at: it's The

Image (and, of course, themselves). Any Image will do; they're all interchangeable. "I'm not living in the real world"? Who is?

My favorite image-junkie story concerns a guy who is not sixteen years old, and apparently harbors no violent or hostile feelings at all. Martha Hume wrote him up in the New York *Daily News*. His name's Kenny, he belongs to the Brotherhood of Teamsters, drives a big rig, and she met him at truckstop in Tennessee, where as a rock journalist she inevitably got around to asking him what kind of music he liked.

"'Well,' Kenny allowed, 'Ah like Willie Nelson and Charlie Daniels and Blondie.'

"Obviously, the lineup amazed me. Willie and Charlie were one thing, but a beer-drinking, two-fisted trucker falling for an 'art rock' band from the nether reaches of Soho—a band that is New Wave, not to say punk? What's going on?

"'I wanna marry her,' explained Kenny.

"'Not *her*,' I wanted to say—but I felt there was no use explaining to Kenny that Blondie is a *band*. Instead, I answered gently, 'I think she lives with her guitar player, Kenny.'

"'Well,' he answered, 'she ain't married is she? As long as she ain't married, it's okay. She can still go out.'

"I realized that Kenny quite seriously felt that 'Blondie' would go for him in a big way if only he could meet her; simultaneously, I realized that Blondie, the band, and Chrysalis, the record company, have pulled off one of the better marketing ploys of the decade."

Did Debbie Re-invent Sex?

A journalist who calls himself Radio Pete writes in *FM* magazine out of L.A.: All new wave bands have a hook—a gimmick—besides the music. At least that's the perception of Chris Stein, lead guitarist for Blondie and husband of the only blonde in the group, Deborah Harry.

'Televisions's aloof, Patti Smith's arty, the Ramones are tough like the army,' Stein says. 'And for our thing ... we have Debbie being sexy. It's like a goof.'

Debbie, on the eve of a headlining Blondie tour of the U.K., to *New Musical Express*: In Britain, we're considered as being just a very successful pop group who don't come on as a threat to anybody ... but God knows ... I really don't know what image they have of me .... It's ludicrous, but I guess it's a pretty subversive one.... I once said jokingly in an interview ... that I wish I had invented sex, so by straight press standards I suddenly became highly controversial .... By American standards, I'm considered pretty wild .... But then, it seems to me that they really desire wanton women over here—so here I am, the new bad girl!

Chrysalis Records magazine ad, ca. '79: pic of Debbie standing in front of a black and white striped wall with her balled fists on her hips, a scornful, scowling, almost dominatrixish look on her face. The rest of the band is visible only in the reproduction of the *Parallel Lines* album cover down in the lower left hand corner, and that's only little larger than a postage stamp, while the ad takes up a full half page. It says: "BLONDIE GIVES GREAT LINES" in bold capital letters across the top, then continues off over on the left side: "Great lines. Great music. Great fun. All put together for your pleasure in one album. The performance is unparalleled. The sound is pop in the purest sense flavored with a heavy dose of gutsy rock 'n' roll. And Deborah Harry delivers a fine set of delicious lines that must be seen now … live."

Whatcha think? Not too sexist? All things considered, right? Certainly a lot better than the ad they ran for one of the band's early singles in all the music papers in England, featuring a photograph of Debbie in a black bodystocking and the giant headline: "WOULDN'T YOU LIKE TO RIP HER TO SHREDS?" I did not make that up. It really happened.

San Francisco New Wave journalist Howie Klein, in *Relix* magazine, June '79, under the headline "Blondie—They're a Group! Not a Girl!" writes: Let's not blame it *all* on the press. Let's look at the promo films and the posters the band (or its representatives) have always had control over. The emphasis is *always* Debbie. The Chrysalis Records press kit, for example, contains five glossy black and white photos—one of Debbie lying on her back in a tee shirt that says 'sex,' one of Debbie looking provocative in a skimpy black one-piece, one of Debbie lounging in cut-offs and a tee shirt, a lips-parted head shot of guess who, and, finally, Debbie with Jimmy, Chris and Clem on the corner of Hollywood and Vine and unlike the first album cover, the boys are in focus on this shot.

Deborah Harry confided her feelings to a woman journalist profiling her for *Penthouse* magazine, mid-1979: I think that the highest appreciation that anyone has is usually sexual …. Just as a girl, as a female, would that bother you?

Yes, admitted the interviewer, if it got in the way of more important things.

Debbie: But that *is* the important thing! …. It really is. Because sex is the biggest seller—sells more magazines, more clothes, more everything. Sex is it, in rock 'n' roll … it's sex and sass …. That 'Ahh, I don't care'—that's a very healthy attitude.

The journalist then asked her what else sells: Debbie ponders for a moment,

scrunching up her face like a little girl. 'Nothing.'

Amazingly enough, out of this flood of newsprint about her, one music magazine actually featured a feminist viewpoint. Under the title "BLONDIE'S Debbie Harry The Hard Way," Karen Davis wrote: 'In the beginning, I tried to stimulate interest in this group in any way that I could,' admits Deborah Harry … 'I used whatever advantages I might have to sell records. Looks have been one of the most saleable things ever. When I woke up to that, mine helped a lot.' Photos of Debbie dressed in a sexy Sheena, Queen of the Jungle outfit began to appear in rock magazines when the group's first album was released around September of 1976. Other photos showed her wearing hot pants and thigh-length boots, or all dolled up in 50's movie starlet gowns, or rolling onstage with her underpants showing. All very Tacky Chic. And it worked. It got Debbie lots of publicity and, along the way, people became vaguely aware that she was part of a rock group.

But once you start using sex appeal as a way of getting attention, it's not always easy to draw the line and have people appreciate your other talents.

'Sometimes that whole image thing can backfire,' admits Debbie. 'There were times when people wound up reviewing how I looked instead of how our music sounded. I suppose lead singers are always singled out initially, particularly because I'm a girl in a group of all guys. It really is obvious. With her 'alluring loveliness,' 'childlike inno-

cence and vast sophistication,' 'cheesecake smile,' 'sensuous pout,' 'sweetness and punk chic,' 'strong sense of humor and self-irony' and her 'huge Chinese take out eyes,' to give just a random sampling of how she's affected some writers who've met her, Debbie kept the spotlights of the world's media focused on the group before they began getting any extensive radio play with their records.

Debbie Harry on feminists, as interviewed by Liz Derringer, *High Times* magazine, November '79:

Do women's libbers ever harass you about being a sex-symbol rock star?

I haven't really run into any heavy butch feminists that have been attacking me, because I think what I do is sort of versatile. I take so many different stances in the music and lyrically that I cover a lot of ground. It's not just as if I'm the weak, feminine creature. I stay away from that lyrically, I don't have that 'Oh, you walked all over me and walk all over me again,' I really don't like that stance anyway.

New York Rocker, mid-'77:

NYR: Chris, is Debbie as vulnerable as she seems?

Chris: More vulnerable than she seems. Nobody realizes the things that affect her. I don't even realize all the things that affect her.

NYR: Do people really accept her image as a "tough girl"?

Chris: No.

New Musical Express, September '79: Debbie: What annoys me is that over here, they try to put girls in one of two categor-ies. Either you're a sweet clean cut girl or a real *nasty* bitch. And, I know which they've figured me out to be.... I got quite turned off myself by all that slush on Farrah Fawcett-Majors ... and I suppose that's precisely the very same thing that was happening with me.

[The "was" in there apparently indicating that now she feels everything is different and under control. If so, when did the change come about? When they got rid of Leeds? When the first tidal wave of superstardom subsided and they all caught their breath? When they found a new, more sympathetic and supportive record company?]

Nashville Tennessean, Nov. 19, 1978: under the headline "Singer Flattered To Be Sex Object," by Jack Williams:

Debbie: It's flattering to be regarded as a sex object. The most recognizable and easiest thing to sell is sex. I'm not the first one to say it or do it.

Melody Maker, mid-'79:

One of the problems with Blondie is that the band were presented as being ultimately just Deborah. You found that annoying, didn't you?

Deborah: It is very annoying. After a certain point, we were sort of getting into it and I was getting most of the attention, until we were hip to what the name of the game was. It was weird and frightening and annoying and insulting, and sometimes it was good, but now it's got to the point where we're taking it and using it to our advantage.

But you do leave yourself open to cheap sensationalism, so it's no use saying you don't want to talk about it after building it up.

Deborah: It is good for us on a commercial level. You've gotta do things like that. I'm not that much of a poseur or an art freak that I'm going to say 'No, no. My art. My art.' This is the business. It's business-art so you have got to use everything you have got to your advantage somehow. It would just be foolish for us to ignore it.

New York Rocker, ca. '76:

'I'm sick of bleaching my hair,' confesses Debbie, 'but I have this feeling of obligation to the band. How could we call ourselves the Blondies if I didn't have blond hair???'

'I think we could change the name,' offers Chris.

Debbie ponders only a moment: 'Ah,' she says, 'I'll keep bleaching it.'

A friend, 1980: They're not good media manipulators, her colorist is! What happened to Lauren Hutton in *American*

Gigolo is gonna happen to Deborah Harry someday. When you bleach your hair that many times it oxydizes and eventually turns green. Someday she's gonna come out of a chlorinated pool and emerge with Kelly Green hair—they'll have to change the name of the group to Kelly!

The Boston Phoenix; under the headline "Blondies Have More Pop," J.D. Considine wrote: One of the best one-liners in pop turned up in 'Look Good in Blue,' from the first Blondie album, where Deborah Harry's sultry voice deadpanned:

I'll give you some head
And shoulders to lie on.

The only thing was, it was a joke about sex that most Americans took to be a sexy joke. Americans, as you might expect of any pop-oriented, media-saturated culture, have a disturbing tendency to take images using sex literally. The fashion model, for example. The idea of sex-as-style can easily be lost in the fascination with sex-as-sex. Despite Deb Harry's coy tongue-in-cheek remarks to the press ('I wish I had invented sex' was one such deadpan taken literally), Blondie as a pop entity have been exclusively concerned with matters like sex-as-style. In fact, the very basis of Blondie-pop seems to be the idea that pop is all form and no content; in other words, cliches as an end in themselves.

Cash Box, February 2, 1980: Blondie is on the cover this week, in living color. The short piece inside congratulates them on climbing so high, so fast, and predicts an even more brilliantined future.

Penthouse: Center stage at New York's Palladium. Debbie stretches, her black bodysuit ripples, glowing. Behind me, a teenager wearing an Iggy T-shirt groans with violent, strained delight.

Deborah, in *Rolling Stone*, December 14, 1978: I'm against the idea that rock stars have to live a life that's completely understandable or predictable to their audience .... There should be a female available for people to have some sort of dream about as a performer, like, 'What is she really like?' Maybe I'll just be the mysterious figure that'll never be able to be truly defined. Maybe that's what my thing is.

Penthouse: 'I've always known how to turn it off and on. I can do it just like that.' She snaps her fingers. 'I'm getting better at it all the time.'

How does Blondie's former producer, Richard Gottehrer, feel on the subject? I asked him: *Do you think there might be a kind of doublethink going on? I know they complained about Private Stock's sexist*

promotion of Blondie and yet they had that picture taken for the pic-disc of Parallel Lines *where she was licking a record.*

Gottehrer: The difference was that maybe *she* chose to do the picture disc, and in the case of the Private Stock thing I don't think it was they were exploiting her sexuality, it was more that it wasn't the way she wanted her sexuality exploited. The poster with the see-thru blouse was done tastefully, but I think what she objected to was at that time they wanted to be and thought of more as a group, she just wasn't ready to accept that sort of photograph. But then look at some of the photos that Chris had taken of her that were run in *Rocker* and in *Punk* magazine that were far more revealing and far sexier, than that. I think maybe she just didn't like the way that photograph happened is all. It's one thing to do something yourself, it's another for somebody to do it without you being part of it.

Chrysalis were the ones that had the ad that said 'Wouldn't You Like to Rip Her to Shreds?,' weren't they?

That was in England.

Didn't the band kick up a big storm about that?

I dunno. Chris said 'Let Blondie Do It To You' and all that was real sexist promotion. [Debbie] once made a point at the beginning, she said, 'When I'm ready to do it my way, then I'll do it.' I think there is nothing wrong with selling this in a sexist way, she is very sexy, attractive, appealing to people, so why not portray it? If she didn't wanna look like that, she wouldn't.

DEBBIE AND CHRIS RAP WITH NEWSMAN JOEL SIEGEL AT CENTRAL PARK CONCERT 1979

Did Chris Re-invent Love?

And everybody's always reasserting how Chris and Debbie are so much in *love*, were in 1973 and are still now today, the relationship having actually survived the love-lethal Seventies where damn few others managed to. So there must be *something* there. But isn't said "love" emotion an absolute contradiction of everything else they're broadcasting? "Love" in pop art? *C'est possible?*

I call Chris Stein.

"It seems to me," I say to him, "that the position you're coming from just is very pretentious. For one thing, I think that your attitude toward the exploitation of Debbie, the sex angle, is either hypocritical or naive, because on one hand you freak out when other people do it yet the way you exploit yourselves—or more precisely, her or she exploits herself—is not that different. Like you said in one interview, 'Well, Debbie's sexuality, that's the hook.'"

"Well," he took a slow deep breath while I panted after that torrent, "I don't know where that statement's from. That's not the attitude around the band, that's for sure. I think Debbie's the victim of a reverse sexism, where because she's a woman in a man's world a lot of people don't like the idea of a girl up there being sexy in front of a lot of men. I think they can accept it from a man in front of women, but it freaks a lot of people out to see a woman in front of men."

"Yeah, but I could say to you by the same token that she plays to sexism by going up there and—"

"Yeah, but so does everybody in rock 'n' roll."

"Not necessarily."

"Sure they do."

"I don't think Talking Heads do."

"They're still attractive, they still try to look good."

"Yeah, but Tina doesn't go up there in a miniskirt with her panties showing."

"Well, I don't care to be compared to Talking Heads at all on any level—I think we're a lot more commercial than them."

"Yeah, but that has nothing to do with sexual exploitation."

"Yeah, but I think we're not any more overtly sexual except it's from a female point of view than any of our contemporaries. Look at Tom Petty, he tries to look as cute as possible. The Clash try to look good, believe me, no matter what they stand for. The Sex Pistols still were sexy to a lot of people."

"Well then why or does it bother you when you see all these magazines with Debbie's picture on the cover?"

"It bothers me when magazines imply that Debbie's prostituting herself and accuse her of overt sexism and then use her picture to sell the paper."

"Yeah, well, I agree with you about that."

"That really burns me, but as far as the media really latching onto Debbie and using her as a visual thing, that doesn't really bother me that much, no. You know, I think she's very attractive. I think that's just natural and happens to anybody who's in that position, it's exactly the same thing that happened to Mick Jagger only it gets exaggerated 'cause Debbie's a girl and he's a guy. But to me the singling out of Mick Jagger and making him into a sex symbol was very similar. It doesn't really go that deep with me. I didn't like some of the things and we had some trouble with the record company, but that's what success brings you.

"Power and freedom. The best parts."

Overleaf:
**THE GANG REHEARSES
AT S.I.R. STUDIO
NEW YORK PRIOR TO
1980 ENGLISH TOUR**

© 1980 H. Strauss

EPILOGUE

After a decade of scuffling, followed by four albums in three years, hits around the world and one song ("Heart of Glass") that might turn out to be an anthem for the emotionally attenuated Seventies, Blondie would seem to be established, even verging on becoming an international pop institution. Curiously, the mood of media paranoia and general grimness the band sometimes gives off somehow belies these otherwise self-evident facts. Maybe they're just going through the usual growing pains—even after ten years of scratching around, their ascendance was vertiginously rapid, and most of the people I talked to, people like Richard Gottehrer and Marty Thau, who've known them for years, seem to feel they will be alright. What I think is that as they gradually develop the self-confidence to stand on the fact that Blondie *is* a group of all-contributing, mutually cooperative songwriter-instrumentalists, the

sexual hype on Debbie (as I write this I am sitting under a Chrysalis poster on a friend's wall emphasizing Debbie in a tight red dress with the slogan "Blondie Does It") will subside and all concerned will be a lot less uptight.

As far as being taken seriously, as "artists," it's always been my perception that art comes in all kinds of forms, and some of the truest artists never have to lean on you to let you know they are. Let it be art. Let it be light and fun; the two are not mutually exclusive, as the Beach Boys could have told you for several years at least. Rock 'n' roll, being a music definitively alive, has always been about growing from the garage into the ability to do and say all the things you want in the ways you want to do and say them, including staying in the garage. There's no reason why, even without some more breaks like the ones they've had so far, this band shouldn't be a thriving pop force in the Eighties.

Photographers

Drawing of Blondie by Hannah Strauss

Photo of Lester Bangs by Fran Pelzman

California born Lester Bangs is a frequent contributor to the *Village Voice, New Musical Express* and other publications around the world. From 1971 to 1976, he worked for *Creem* magazine where he created a style of mutant critical-journalism based on the sound and language of rock 'n' roll which has influenced many writers and musicians. As a musician/composer, he has led two bands active on the Manhattan club scene, singing lead, playing the harmonica and presenting original compositions. His first recorded single, "Let It Blurt/Live" was released on the Spy label in 1979. In the works is *Rock Gomorrah* (A Delilah Book) co-authored with Michael Ochs.